Simple Elegant Napkins

Simple Elegant Napkins

Avril O'Donnell

Over 50 ideas for a stylish table

NEW HOLLAND

To Stephen and my family

First published in 2006 by
New Holland Publishers (UK) Ltd
London • Cape Town • Sydney • Auckland
www.newhollandpublishers.com

Garfield House
86-88 Edgware Road
London W2 2EA
United Kingdom

80 McKenzie Street
Cape Town 8001
South Africa

14 Aquatic Drive
Frenchs Forest, NSW 2086
Australia

218 Lake Road
Northcote, Auckland
New Zealand

ISBN 1 84537 243 3

Editor: Ruth Hamilton
Designer: Gülen Shevki-Taylor
Photographer: Stuart West
Photographic stylist: Avril O'Donnell
Production: Hazel Kirkman
Editorial direction: Rosemary Wilkinson

10 9 8 7 6 5 4 3 2 1

Reproduction by Pica Digital PTE Ltd, Singapore
Printed and bound by Times Offset (M) Sdn Bhd, Malaysia

Contents

Introduction

The use of napkins and napkin rings can transform the look of your table, whether you are hosting an informal supper or a more structured dinner party. Use the ideas in this book to inject some fun, elegance and colour into any dining occasion. Be as creative as you like and enjoy choosing your fabrics, styles and accessories!

The folding of napkins can range from the very basic to the more complex. In this book I have kept the folding fairly simple yet elegant and with the added use of napkin rings you can achieve some very stylish results.

Special occasions, such as a wedding, are the perfect time to use napkins to enhance your table decorations. There are plenty of ideas to choose from in the book, whatever the occasion. Pick colours and fabrics to go with your theme and choose napkin folds and napkin rings to co-ordinate. Be creative and make your table decorations as special as your day! There are many other special celebrations such as birthdays, anniversaries or Valentine's Day when you may wish to use one of the design ideas in this book. Seasonal ideas are also included, from Christmas dinner to summer alfresco dining, which are all excellent opportunities to experiment with napkin folding and presentation.

There may be other times when napkins can be used, for example, to complement the setting for an occasion with a theme. For an Indian or Chinese meal, whether you are cooking yourself or ordering in, the table can be dressed with the appropriate crockery and finished by using a suitable napkin design.

Table napkins can be used to make even the simplest meal unique and ensure that your extra special meals are just perfect.

Handy Information

When buying new napkins one of the main considerations will be the type of fabric you require. If you are buying for long term use, choose a more expensive fabric such as linen or good quality cotton, which will keep its appearance for a long period of time. As an alternative, you could buy a selection of cheaper napkins in different colours, patterns and fabrics to match any dining occasion.

There are also many new fabrics from which to choose, such as voile, organza, silver shot linen, or highly glittered and embroidered fabrics. These are all very exciting and will give you a large variety of looks and ideas for your dining table.

When choosing the fabric the end design should be kept in mind. Heavier fabrics such as linen, damask or embossed materials will suit the more structured designs as these will fold well and stand up if necessary. The finer materials will be more suitable for softer designs that are tucked into a glass or gathered in a napkin ring. The different fabrics in this book have been chosen to suit particular napkin designs, although there are some designs that will work with many materials.

For more structured and crisply folded designs starching would be useful, either in the washing process or by using a spray-on starch.

Before attempting any type of napkin design, a good pressing with an iron is essential to the finished look. Some designs will benefit from ironing as you go along to keep the folds in position and this will give a neater finish to your napkin.

If your white napkins are looking a little tired, try using a whitening washing solution and spray with a linen spray to give a nice scent. Alternatively, you could dye the napkins another colour for a new lease of life.

When using napkins frequently, which I'm sure you will after reading this book, use easy-care fabrics which can be quickly cleaned in the machine and require little ironing.

NAPKIN FOLDS

There is a napkin fold suitable for every occasion, whether you want something classic and elegant or colourful and funky. The folds in this chapter range from simple designs for picnics and informal lunches through to more structured folds for formal dinner parties. Advice on material and suitable occasions to present your napkin folds are given for each design so you can make the most of your creativity.

The Flute

Beautiful rich jewel colours in fabrics such as a light organza or voile would make an outstanding contrast to an otherwise white table setting. For a wedding try to co-ordinate colours with the flowers or the bridesmaid dresses.

1 Take the napkin and diagonally gather it towards the centre.

2 Tie a fairly tight knot just over half way down the napkin.

3 Take a champagne flute and push the knot to the bottom of the glass. Pull the long end of the napkin up straight and arrange the shorter end over the glass.

Picnic Pocket

As the name suggests, this would be ideal for picnics or alfresco dinners as the napkins can be prepared in advance and placed on the table at the last minute. Soft cottons in bright colours, checks and prints work well with this design.

1 Fold the napkin in half diagonally, then in half again to make a triangle.

2 Starting at one narrow point roll up loosely, leaving space for cutlery.

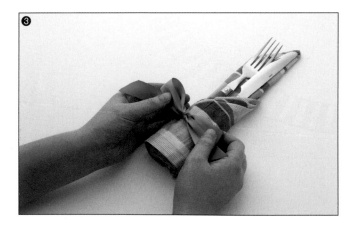

3 Place your cutlery in between the folds. Either leave the ends just folded underneath or use a piece of colourful ribbon to keep everything in place.

Crossroads

The key to this modern design is the clean and simple lines that are created. Present it at formal or casual dinner parties and use cotton or linen fabrics. A single flower or stem enhances the effect.

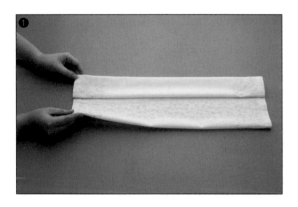

1 Fold the napkin in half lengthways. Fold the top and bottom edges to the centre of the napkin.

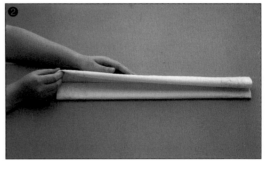

2 Fold up the bottom edge again then fold the top edge down to lay on top of it. You should have a flat, even strip.

3 Lay the strip with the open side of the fold facing away from you. Place your hand in the centre and fold down the right side at 45 degrees. Then take the left side and cross it over the right.

Popsicle

Choose this design for a barbecue or picnic when you can use bright colourful prints in a fun way. Use easycare fabrics which can be popped into the washing machine at the end of the day.

1 Fold the napkin in half, then in half again to make a square.

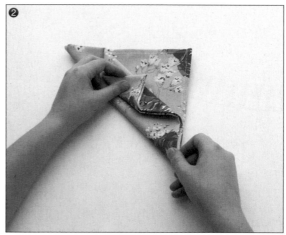

2 Take one corner and fold it up to the opposite corner, fold back down two thirds and then back up again in half. The folded point should now face the opposite corner.

3 Now fold the napkin in half so that the folds are on the outside. Pick up the napkin, making sure you have hold of all the folds and place in a glass. Arrange the points at the top of the napkin.

Chopstick Roll

This is a very simple idea that uses a black linen napkin. A cotton fabric would work just as well in any plain colour. You can use this fold to add a touch of the orient to a Chinese meal by including chopsticks.

1 Place your chopsticks next to the napkin, then fold the napkin until it is about 4 in (10 cm) longer than the chopsticks.

2 With the fold uppermost, start to roll the napkin towards one end, making it about 2 in (5 cm) wide.

3 Place your chopsticks on top on the roll and tie in place with a length of thin ribbon.

Valentine

This heart shaped design is such a pretty shape it could be used for any romantic meal. The gorgeous stiff organza has almost dictated the type of fold to be chosen and the use of the tassel to hold it in place is an essential part of the design.

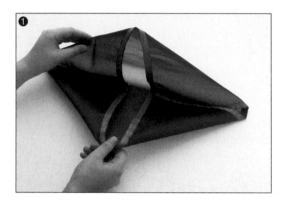

1 Fold all four corners to the centre. Then fold in half to form a triangle. Turn the base of the triangle towards you.

2 Take the bottom two corners and fold them up towards the centre point. Fold the napkin in half down the centre gully between the two triangles.

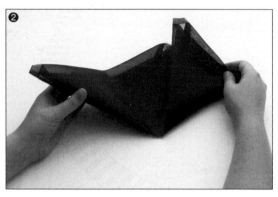

3 Take hold of all the top points together and turn to face you. Secure the points with a tie, such as a tassel. Arrange the napkin on its side and pull out the wings into a soft heart shape.

Angel Wing

This graceful napkin fold would look lovely at any occasion, but would particularly suit a wedding or formal dinner party. Use cotton or linen fabrics to get the best effect.

1 Fold the napkin in half diagonally, making sure the corners match up evenly.

2 Repeat step 1. Then take the right hand side of the napkin and fold it down the middle of the napkin.

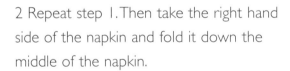

3 Take the other side of the napkin and wrap it over the front to make a conical shape. Leave the ends of the napkin tucked round the back of the cone.

Portfolio

Another modern design for your dining table, this chic and elegant style will enhance any table setting. Most fabrics are suitable for this fold but cotton or linen will work best if you want a nice crisp finish.

1 Lay the napkin out flat, fold each corner to the centre then flip the napkin over. Take the top corner and fold to the centre then repeat with the bottom corner.

2 Fold the right hand edge two-thirds of the way over to the left, then fold it back on itself so the point is level with the side.

3 Finally, take the left point and fold it over the right point, making sure you don't cover it completely.

The Flame

Any soft, printed fabric would work well for this design, so why not use it for a themed evening? A really decorative and special napkin ring would really set this fold off perfectly.

1 Fold the napkin into a triangle, then fold again into a smaller triangle. Do not match the corners on the second fold, but off-set by about 1¼ in (3 cm).

2 Fold again into a smaller triangle, again not matching the corners by about 1¼ in (3 cm). The triangle should look stepped.

3 Concertina from the folded corner, then slip a napkin ring over the end and ease it towards the centre. Finally, fan out the points to resemble a flame.

Centrepoint

As this is such a smart modern shape, this napkin is ideal for dinner parties when you want to impress your guests. Use fabrics such as linen, cotton or damask and make sure you use starch to get a really sharp finish.

1 Fold the napkin in half, then take the folded end and turn up by about 1½ in (4 cm). Turn the napkin over.

2 Have the napkin with the hemmed edges facing away from you. Fold up the bottom right hand corner to the centre and repeat with the left corner. You should now have a triangle shape.

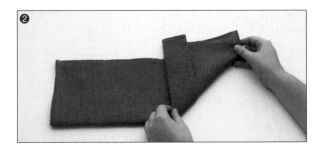

3 Fold the triangle in half in between the folds. Stand it up by spreading the bottom edges of the napkin out to create feet.

Parchment Roll

This is napkin folding in its most basic form and would be suitable for any occasion, whether formal or casual. You can prepare your napkins in advance and place on the table at the last minute. Most fabrics can be used for this fold.

1 Fold the napkin in half, then in half again, to form a square.

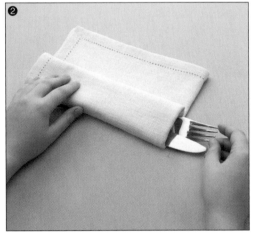

2 Add cutlery at this point if you wish. Roll up the napkin – if your napkin has a decorative edge then start rolling from the opposite end so you can show it off.

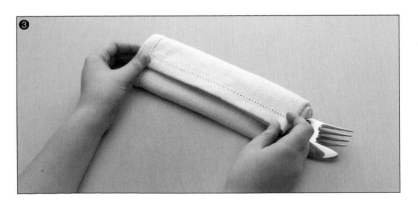

3 Place the napkin at the table setting. Either leave with the decorative edge showing or turn it over and tuck the edges underneath for a smooth finish.

Emperor's Sail

This rich and sumptuous fold allows the napkin to stand either on the table or on a side plate. Linen and damask fabrics are perfect for this and double-sided napkins with a printed and a coloured side will also look great.

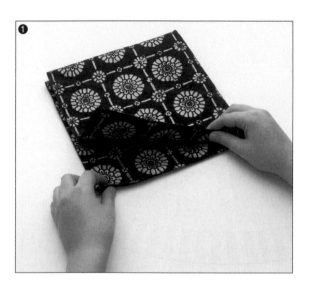

1 Fold the napkin in half, then in half again to make a square.

2 Peel back three layers of the fabric and fold the remaining corner back under the napkin.

3 Pull up all but the bottom layer and take the two side corners round to meet at the back. This will make a shape resembling a sail. Separate the layers to show off the coloured underside of the napkin.

Oyster Shell

Use this napkin fold in a formal setting, ideally with a fabric that has a really strong design or print that you can show off. Linen and cotton mixes suit this design as the fabric needs to be fairly stiff.

1 Have the napkin lying reverse side up. Fold over two corners to the middle.

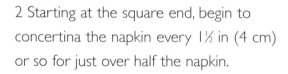

2 Starting at the square end, begin to concertina the napkin every 1½ in (4 cm) or so for just over half the napkin.

3 Flip the pointed end under to make the last concertina, this should leave about 4 in (10 cm) of the triangle out. Place your finger in the middle of the napkin and fold over to make a leaning fan shape.

The Roxy

This glamorous style was inspired by the glitzy musical extravaganzas of the 1940s. Use rich and opulent fabrics like organza which creates a lovely, sparkly effect. This fold will need some starching to get it to stand up well.

1 Fold the napkin in half lengthways. Concertina the fabric every 1¼ in (3 cm) from one short end. Iron the pleats as you go for a crisp finish.

2 Place your finger in the middle of the napkin and twist the pleats around in opposite directions to form a circular shape.

3 Hold the front of the pleats and fold the back fan upwards. To make this stand properly you may need to fold back the bottom of the rear fan.

Square Dance

This compact and stylish design is ideal for lunch or dinner with friends and is perfect for use on a smaller table. Use heavy fabrics such as 100% cotton, linen or damask and starch before you start the fold.

1 Using a large napkin, fold the napkin in half.

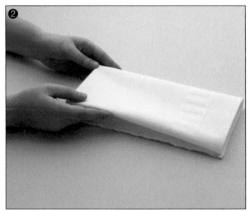

2 Fold the napkin in half again, and then in half again, to make a small rectangle.

3 Finally, fold the napkin in half again to make a small square. Pick up the loose corners and stand them up in the middle of the napkin. The heavy fabrics used will make this easier, as will using a spray starch.

Pop Top

Add some fun to your summer table with this design which is great for boldly patterned or colourful napkins. Use fabrics that are lightweight and easy to care for.

1 Have the napkin right side up. Fold the napkin in half lengthways and then fold a quarter back on itself to reveal the correct side.

2 Concertina the napkin every 2¾-3¼ in (7-8 cm) in one direction, to create a stepped effect.

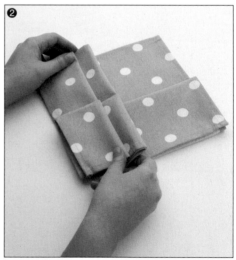

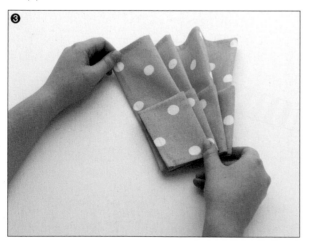

3 Tuck the last piece of fabric around the back of the steps and slightly fan out the top.

Petticoat Tails

This pretty and feminine design is suitable for a special occasion. The fold works wonderfully well with a lace napkin that lets the light filter through. Choose a napkin ring of your choice and use starch to help the napkin stand well.

1 Fold the napkin from corner to corner to form a triangle shape.

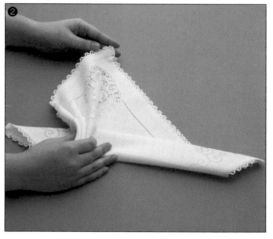

2 Fold up about 2 in (5 cm) from the bottom of the triangle. Concertina the napkin from the centre, working outwards evenly.

3 While holding the gathers together push your napkin ring over the bottom of the napkin and ease into place. Arrange the top of the napkin so that it is neat and even.

Rose Swirl

Try this fold when you want to create a fabulous design with very little effort. Choose fabrics which are soft and easy to gather, such as cotton and polyester mixes. A plain coloured napkin would show off this design best.

1 Lay your napkin over a side plate, correct side facing upwards.

2 Using your thumb and finger pinch the centre of the napkin and start to twist in one direction until most of the napkin is swirled.

3 You will start to see a rose shape in the centre of the napkin. Ease the centre out a little and arrange the edges of the napkin in soft folds.

The Scroll

Richly embossed fabrics, such as damask in cream or white, would be suitable for this scroll. It is elegant yet simple to fold and the corded tassel gives a beautiful finishing touch.

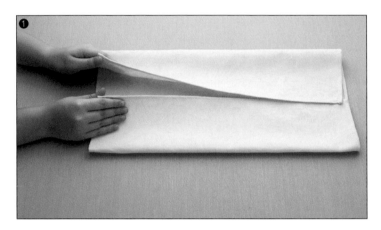

1 Fold the top and bottom edges to meet in the centre.

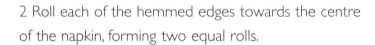

2 Roll each of the hemmed edges towards the centre of the napkin, forming two equal rolls.

3 Place the corded tassel around the centre of the napkin and tie in a loose knot. Finally, tease out the inner rolls at the top to form a scroll.

Dragonfly

Use a napkin ring of your choice to hold this napkin in place – try and co-ordinate it with the napkin and your table settings. We have used a stunning silver shot linen fabric that will catch the light with a beautiful dragonfly ring.

1 Starting from the centre of the napkin, and working diagonally, fold under about 1½ in (4 cm) of the fabric. Continue towards the corner.

2 Repeat step 1 on the other side of the napkin. Fold one half of the pleated napkin on top of the other half. Tuck the corners underneath.

3 Fold one end of the napkin over towards the other end – but not quite in half. Place a ring over the pleats and pull out the bottom to reveal a corner point.

Double Twist

This is a great way of updating an existing plain napkin, by introducing a new colour or print you can get a completely different look for your dining table. This is suitable for most types of fabrics but starching will give a good finish to the fold.

1 Take both napkins and fold them into triangles. Place one of top of the other, slightly offset.

2 Start to roll from one end to the other. To help get a good shape you can use a rolling pin to wrap them around.

3 A two tone effect is now achieved. Either lay the napkin on the table and tease out the bottom rolls or, if you have used starch, you can stand the twist up.

Chrysler Point

A smart, chic design like this is great for special occasions where you want to impress your guests. It looks professional, but is very simple to achieve if you use a crisp cotton or linen fabric.

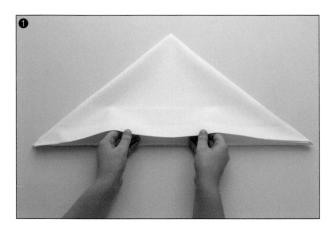

1 Fold the napkin into a triangle, then again into a smaller triangle.

2 Start to fold the napkin into steps from the centre. This will form a zig-zag effect at the top of the napkin.

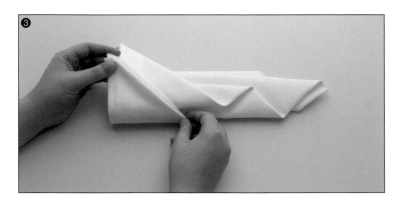

3 Take the other side of the napkin and fold it back along the centre, leaving about ¾ in (2 cm) showing. Then wrap both ends around the napkin to sit across the bottom edge.

Pizza Roll

This is a classically simple design that can be used for any occasion. Try using one of the decorative ideas in the Napkin Rings chapter to add interest. Use a cotton mix fabric to achieve the best results with this fold.

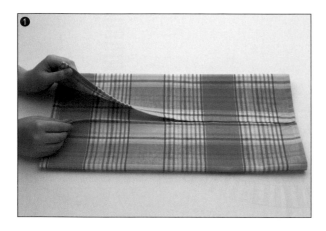

1 Take the napkin and fold down the top edge to the centre, then fold the bottom edge up so that both edges meet in the middle.

2 Start to roll up the napkin from one short end, making it slightly conical. Make sure the end of the roll is tucked underneath.

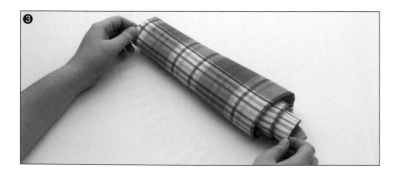

3 Place the napkin on the table and tease out the ends of the rolls to form steps.

Cascade

A soft and romantic style for evenings when dining by candlelight. This design could also be placed in a glass or be cascading from a bowl if you wish. Use fabrics from the new range of organdies, voiles and man-made polyesters.

1 Fold the napkin in half diagonally to make a triangle.

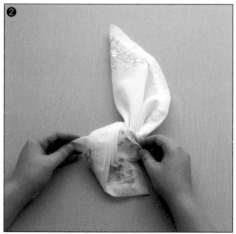

2 Gather the napkin from the long edge up to the top point. Hold in place, take the tails behind and tie in a loose knot.

3 Carefully slide the knot into position. Arrange the tails into a pretty shape and ease out the folds of the knot.

Simple Cone

This sweet and simple napkin design is ideal for everyday use, both for smart dinners and alfresco dining. Most fabrics are suitable and you can use any type of print or colour to match your table settings.

1 Fold the napkin in half, then in half again to make a square.

2 Take one corner and fold it up towards the opposite corner, leaving it short by about 5 cm.

3 Take the right and left corners and fold them to the middle of the napkin, keeping the angles even. Turn the napkin over and place on the table. You can put your hand inside the cone to raise the centre slightly for a three dimensional look.

NAPKIN RINGS

Choosing a napkin ring to set off your napkin fold design allows you to let your imagination run free! Use rings, ribbons, flowers, beads and decorations to create co-ordinating rings that will complement your table settings. This chapter is split into different themes and occasions to give you masses of inspiration for making your own napkin rings. Use these ideas as a jumping-off point for your own creations.

Classic Wedding

This is the perfect time to decorate your napkins. Choose colours and materials to suit a theme and take inspiration from ribbons, buttons and flowers used in the wedding. These ideas will help you create some really pretty napkin rings.

1 This beautiful ribbon trimming is perfect to use all by itself. Cut a piece of about 7 in (18 cm), place around the napkin and stitch the two ends together at the back.

2 These pearls were bought as a necklace, then trimmed down to a suitable length. The ends were carefully tied so the pearls won't fall off. Wrap them around The Scroll (page 48) and tie in place with some thread or a small piece of wire.

3 Making your own rings can really add that personal touch. For example, use buttons that match the buttons on the bride's dress. Sew them on to one end of a strip of ribbon and make button holes in the other end to secure them in place.

4 Pretty wire-stemmed fabric flowers have been used here by entwining the stems around each other to form a circle. Perhaps you could match them to the flowers that were used in the bride's bouquet.

Modern Wedding

For a more up-to-date and glamorous look, use sheer fabrics and glitzy accessories that will catch the light. Use sparkly silver, gold and diamanté in simple designs to create a really modern feel to the occasion.

1 Try using ivory ribbon; this is about 1⅓ in (3.5 cm) wide and 8 in (20 cm) long. The centrepiece is a sparkling diamanté buckle. Simply feed the ribbon through the buckle and tie it in a knot at the back of a napkin fold such as The Scroll (page 48).

2 This napkin ring has a duel purpose, both as a decorative item and also as a wedding favour. This gold pouch was bought, but you can easily sew your own and add it to the romantic fold, Cascade (page 58).

3 An alternative to plain ribbon is one with an elegant cut-out design. Simply wrap the ribbon around the napkin and secure at the back by sewing or with glue.

4 Wired ribbon is widely available in craft shops and haberdasheries. Simply tie a piece around the napkin and finish with a bow, arranging the tails prettily.

Ethnic

Inspired by Mexican culture, these ideas can be used any time and are suitable for formal dinners, lunch with friends or a barbecue. Use rich earthy colours and textured napkins together with beautiful beads and ties.

1 A tassel can be a very effective napkin ring. All you need to do is tie it in place at the desired point on the napkin. We have also used an interesting little feather as an additional decoration to a Parchment Roll (page 32).

2 Unique handmade beads can be bought from many craft shops. Simply thread them onto a length of leather shoelace in any order and tie at the back.

3 This is an interesting idea with uses a length of leather shoelace and a large decorative bead. Thread the bead onto the middle of the shoelace, then wrap the lace round the napkin several times and tie at the back.

4 Use old beaded bracelets or necklaces. Take them apart and thread the beads onto some wire in a new order. Bend and crimp the ends of the wire so that the beads don't slip off and the wire can't scratch, then wrap the ring around the napkin.

Christmas

This is a great occasion to make your own elegant napkin rings. You may already have Christmas decorations that you could use as rings. Try colours such as gold, red and green to match the season and use really special napkin fabrics.

1 This bought wired sprig of stars looks equally good on a white napkin as it does on this gauzy gold fabric. Use a rolling pin to wrap the sprig around, arranging the wires as you go to get a good shape.

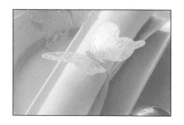

2 For a look that is so simple to achieve take a Christmas decoration off your tree (as long as it is not too big) and just loop it around your napkin. You could have a different one for each place setting.

3 Use a pre-wired branch or sprig of leaves with a bit of sparkle to them. Just cut off the amount you require and bend around to make a circle shape. Be careful not to have sharp wires sticking out.

4 These white glitter butterflies are ideal to make into rings as they are already on wire stems. Use a rolling pin to wrap the wire around then just twist the ends together to fix at the back.

Valentine

Valentine's Day is a fabulous excuse for using beautiful and glamorous napkin rings. Use whites, reds and pinks in the napkins and rings and try to find accessories with hearts and flower symbols to set off the theme.

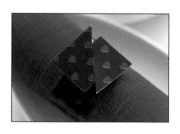

1 For this idea we have used a key-ring with a loveheart motif. Simply slip the ring over the end of the napkin fold, such as The Flame (page 28). You can use different key-ring motifs for any dinner party, as long as the ring is big enough.

2 This simple idea uses some pretty red ribbon to wrap around a plain white napkin. For a special touch use bought decorations, like these feather butterflies, to place on a formal fold such as the Chrysler Point (page 54).

3 Cut a 1¼ x 8¼ in (3 x 21 cm) strip of pretty card. Make a diagonal cut, 1¼ in (3 cm) in from one end, to halfway across the width. Repeat for the other end, on the opposite side, then wrap around the napkin and slot the diagonal cuts together.

4 This pretty ready-made trim with rosebuds can be wrapped twice around a white napkin and finished at the back by sewing the ends together.

Party

Ideas for decorating napkins for parties can be as exciting as you would like them to be! Use your imagination, be creative and surprise your guests with unusual designs. Colours can be co-ordinated to any other party decorations.

1 Buy some fake-fur trimming to loop around your napkins. Use a simple fold such as the Parchment Roll (page 32) and tie or stitch at the back to hold in place. This is a fun design which will really amuse your guests.

2 Cut a piece of white cotton broderie anglaise slightly longer than you need to wrap around the napkin. Thread it with some narrow co-ordinating or matching ribbon, wrap around the napkin, tie the ribbon and arrange the gathers neatly.

3 Use colourful, sparkly or shiny ribbon to simply coil around your napkin. Leave the ends to tumble onto the plate or table.

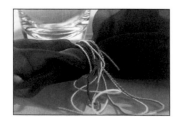

4 Finding unusual ways to decorate your table is part of the fun of hosting a dinner party to remember. In this case we have used some curly wires in bright colours which have been wound around the napkin.

Alfresco

Liven up your napkins for summer dining by using some of these bright ideas, which are all easy to do. Use exiting colours and textures and have fun being creative! You could also use some of these ideas for a children's birthday party.

1 For this design we have used ready-made wired paper flowers. They normally come as individual sprigs so we have entwined a few stems together to form a ring.

2 Use ready-made trimmings such as these daisies to make a really funky napkin ring. Wrap the daisies around as many times as you like and put a stitch in the back to hold it in place.

3 Use edible candy necklaces which you can buy from sweet shops. Wrap the necklace around a simple napkin roll, such as Pizza Roll (page 56). Kids will love to take these away at the end of the meal!

4 Looking round craft shops provides lots of inspiration. Brightly coloured beads were slipped on to a piece of ribbon and tied around the napkin. Guests could also take them away as little bracelets.

Fresh Flowers

Decorating your napkins with flowers or foliage is a very quick and effective way to create a theme, whether it is a wedding, barbecue or Valentine's Day. Use flowers with a lovely scent to enhance a special occasion.

1 Heather has been used here as a delightful alternative to a flower. Simply cut a few stems about 8 cm long then secure in place with a matching coloured ribbon.

2 To have a lovely scent at the table why not use a herb, such as rosemary? Lay a sprig on The Scroll (page 48) and use a length of trailing ivy to secure by twisting around the napkin and tying in a knot.

3 A miniature red rose provides an exquisite contrast to a white table setting. Lay it in the centre of your napkin roll and use a shoelace ribbon to tie in place with a bow.

4 Use a vibrant colour such as this pink gerbera. We have tucked it into the Chrysler Point (page 54) and used a ribbon to decorate. Either tie the ribbon around the napkin or simply drape it over the plate.

Acknowledgements

The author and publishers would like to thank the following shops for their assistance in supplying props to be used in this book:

Cath Kidston
51 Marylebone High Street
London W1U 5HW
Tel: 0207 935 6555
www.cathkidston.co.uk

The Pier
200 Tottenham Court Road
London W1T 7PL
Tel: 0207 637 7001
www.pier.co.uk

Itzomi
20 Lower Kings Road
Berkhamstead
Herts HP4 2AB
Tel: 01442 878939
www.itzomi.co.uk

The Old Wool Shop
29 High Street
Tring
Herts HP23 5AA
Tel: 01442 827979